GHA   ʹ
HOLIDAYS

DAVID WILLIAMS

First published in 2019
by Oort Publications
London United Kingdom SW17

Designed and typeset by Jon Langridge
Printed in England in the United Kingdom

ISBN 978-1-5272-4254-8

GHASTLY HOLIDAYS

things my father never told me...

Ghastly Holidays captures the truly awful things that can and probably have beset us all. No - not just missed flights, dog chewed passports, or one of the children setting off a full airport security alert with another unmentionable piercing, no, Ghastly Holidays is about remembering all those good times, possibly because they were bloody awful. In fact, have you ever been on holiday without incident? Ghastly Holidays might remind you of a few of these times, and the utter relief we can feel returning home.

oort
PUBLICATIONS

David Williams is a surveyor and has been at the same firm since 1982 where he started in the marketing department 'prepping' the advertisements for Country Life. From Harrow School, he went straight to work and now assists owners and developers deliver their dream schemes around the world.

A trustee of The Caerhays Estate in Cornwall, David lives in London and has many passions including common sense, an inexorable appetite for life, cricket, Wimbledon Common, Cornwall and ABF The Soldiers' Charity.

With thanks to the family for the ideas and God
for the elixir of rosé.

In memory of Julian Williams; the kindest father one could wish for
and
Henry Angell-James; the brightest surveyor you may have been
lucky enough to meet.

Also published by the same author:

FILTHY CREATURES

To be published by the same author:

BUFFY'S BEAUTIES
SHOCKING STARS

...other stuff to follow

"The finest travel companion to have along with rosé and a cigar."
— JONATHAN AND JEMMA HEWLETT

"We will fight Williams on the beaches."
— A DISTANT RELATIVE OF WINSTON

"David Williams – Roald Dahl on rosé."
— DIGBY FLOWER

"Mad, bad and dangerous.
After copious amounts of rosé: entertaining."
— KATIE BOSCAWEN

"The incomparable David Williams does it again! Ghastly Holidays
cannot fail to make you smile – a breath of fresh air in such a
serious world."
— ROSEANNA JAGGARD

"From one of the great social commentators of the 21st century
on the absolute necessity of a permanent supply of rosé
when on holiday."
— SARAH BANHAM

"Some people think it's funny but it's really rather runny – another
solid read from DW."
— STEVE ALDERSON

"They seek him here, they seek him there, That David Williams
is everywhere!"
— SALLY ANGELL-JAMES

"David Williams is quite simply a modern day guru. That he can write poetry overflowing with deep emotional insight is a welcome if almost inevitable bonus to his many enthusiastic followers – including us!"
— CHARLES AND DONNA SCOTT

"After reading David's previous book, who could not order at least ten copies of this new one; another truly amazing read and classic."
— ROGER MADELIN

"Faulty Towers meets hilarious Belloc."
— PETER FREEMAN

"A deliciously absurd selection of poems by a deliciously absurd poet – long may he carry on in the same vein." (Oorthor's note – wait for Buffy's Beauties)
— ROBERT WOLSTENHOLME

"An immensely entertaining voyage through family life... His poems offer an eclectic, ironic and funny glimpse into the world we are lucky enough to live in."
— LISA CARTER

"This book should be seen as an amusing warning of what will happen if you take a holiday with this lunatic."
— SIMON STONE

"A great reminder of how to (largely) enjoy oneself."
— SIMON WATERFIELD

GHASTLY HOLIDAYS

HURRAY FOR ROSÉ

People pay for the cirque du soleil,
But I prefer rosé,
People say "olé le Moet"
Non, je préfère rosé.

Un petit filet, avec cafe au lait?
Actually I prefer rosé,
Peut-être le coq in an old bidet?
No, even screw top rosé's OK.

Perhaps a roll in an old duvet?
Non; je dit rosé,
Mais avec mois coucher to-day?
Non; c'est parfait de rosé.

Monsieur, peut-être le gâteau foret?
Look dear chap whatever you say,
You are simply not au fait,
With the fact: je t'aime le rosé!

MORAL *A rosé a day, c'est parfait!*

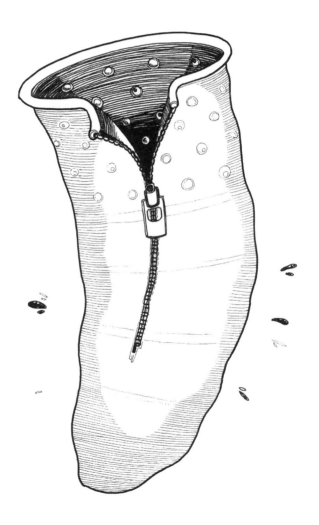

LIVING RUBBER

Rubber has all kinds of uses,
Conjuring up carnal abuses,
"Hang on Darling, just hold that moment,
I'm going to fumble about and make myself impotent."

Let's not forget, what comes down goes up it,
So there is no need to act like a muppet,
If you're short of some and feeling ripe,
Why not try a bit of old hosepipe?

Another use which will make you catch your breath,
Is how people use it at New Polzeath.
In an act of living rubber devotion,
People plunge into the Atlantic Ocean,
Attaching a huge board to their feet and ankles,
Paddling out to sea in these fluorescent manacles.

Once done up and securely zipped,
Nothing gets in or out; that's really it,
Goodness knows what you do,
With a fully engaged and rather runny number two?

Then if you're feeling slightly sinister,
You can always board over your Prime Minister,
Frankly I'd prefer a much simpler death,
Than to drown in the black rubber flotsam that is New Polzeath.

MORAL *"Used to rubber but its sore all over now."*

HOW TO DRIVE GREEK

A driving test is not required,
Insurance a flight of fancy,
A surface road is undesired,
Indicators are for nancies.

Mirrors are merely decorative,
To assist in personal preening,
They have no further part to play,
And yes, they have no meaning.

Drive hard at oncoming vehicles,
Preferably in the middle of the road,
There's no point in wearing spectacles,
Although worth building in a commode.

A parking space is meaningless,
Just stop exactly where you want,
It's meant to cause uneasiness,
And ensure you call out ....!

The quickest way to meet your maker,
Is to become a blind summit over taker,
The more acute the angle, the greater the danger,
A much greater chance of killing a perfect stranger.

Finally the greatest machine,
There has ever been,
Is of course the redoubtable quad bike.
Difficult to steer,
Without 14 beers,
It can throw you off when
you like.

MORAL *Hire a boat.*

HUMMING BIRD

Mouths can start talking free of the brain,
As befits Alzheimer's,
There's no humming and erring, just another refrain,
Outbursts are as welcome as silence.

Not so the humming bird, the Trochilidae,
In flight their hums and errs are incessant,
As fast backwards as forwards, so easy to fly,
With a wingbeat a hundred times a second.

Another amazing trick to make you look,
They can nest on a tiny rubber hook,
And perhaps as a mother does after a spat with her daughter,
Become a humming bird, spend ninety percent of your life in torpor.

In size as small as a honey bee,
A tongue half the size of its body,
No wonder they get into night clubs for free,
To pour themselves a small triple voddy.

MORAL *A hummer is worth waiting for.*

THE ONLY BUS IN LOSIERES

There is only one bus in Losieres,
No chance of them coming in pairs,
Certainly not in threes and fours,
Non, zut alors!

Mademoiselle Diesel vin de Creuts,
Is the name of this charming autobus,
Like some old girls she's got a smelly engine,
Taking sole focus on picking up Frenchmen.

One of her particular dislikes,
In addition to anyone on bikes,
Are Englishmen who come and pet her,
She'll simply swallow you up in her carburettor.

There's no point in reading timetables,
You may as well read Aesop's Fables,
Autobus sept, à dix heures moins le quart,
Is probably a bus time on Mars.

An attempt was made in 1864,
To supplement Madame's services with her daughter-in-law,
But Madame is rumoured to have forced,
Thirteen light bulbs up her nieces exhaust.

And so dear reader if you ever find a bus,
Just turn around without a fuss,
Forget it, she isn't worth stalking,
It's so much better walking.

MORAL *Dis non, to publique transport.*

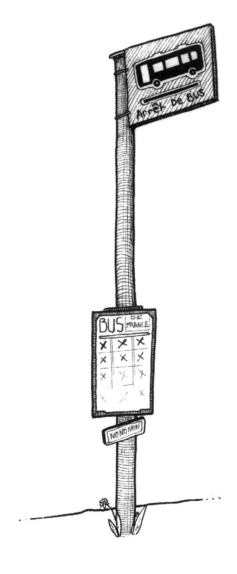

ROSIE

HALF CORGI; HALF ALSATIAN

When a friend says; "Oh, could you have my dog,
It's only for a couple of days?"
You never know what you're going to get,
Does it bark all night or laze?

"Rosie, she's called; half Corgi, half Alsatian,"
The visions going through one's head,
She's going to send us to eternal damnation.

Rosie's mother left and closed the door,
Rosie frowned and started whining,
As foodie smells splashed across the floor,
"Thank God!" she said, "I require fine dining."

Our first meeting was I'm told atypical,
She had climbed up nesting on the sofa,
Fluffing up the cushions around her,
To raise herself above us mere gofers.

"I'd like my mummy back,
And your food is crap,"
Were her first cordial greetings,
"And yes, I see you stare,
Because I have one ear,
Please turn on your central heating's."

Day one began at an imperious low,
Day two proved slightly better,
Days three to five were just so-so,
And on day six we received a letter...,
"Dear Sara, David and whoever,
Thanks for having me to Westover,
The black dogs will just have to go,
If you ever want me back over."

MORAL *Rosie you are always welcome.*

DAY TRIP LONDON

Taxi
Tube Victoria
Train Clapham Junction
Train Epsom
Train Waterloo
Tube Canning Town
DLR Silvertown
DLR Canning Town
DLR Beckton
DLR Canning Town
Tube Waterloo
Train Clapham Junction
Train East Croydon
Train Clapham Junction

MORAL *Bravo pubic transport.*

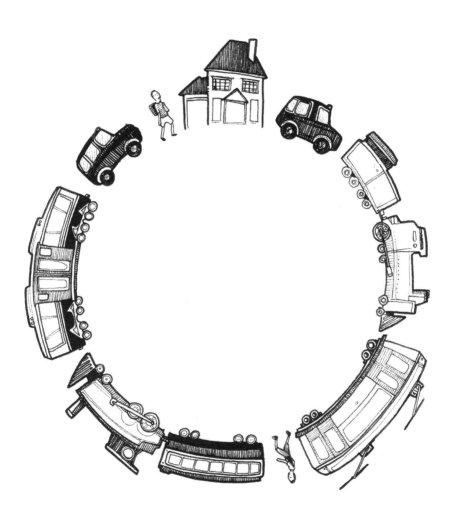

"WHERE HAVE YOU BEEN THIS WEEKEND?"
MRS WILLIAMS

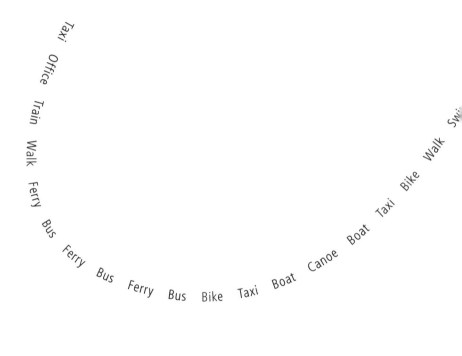

Bike Walk Bus Ferry Bus Ferry Bus Ferry Bus Ferry Taxi Plane Bus Shuttle Train Tube Office

MORAL *Weekend round trip to Muckle Flugga and The Old Stack.*

(Capped by a largish lady puffing and panting, pushing a pram onto the train at Gatwick saying; "Do you realise I've had to push this pram all the way from the airport?!" "Well done madam.")

WELCOME TO GRIMAUD

There are few pretences,
That amongst the Hewlett residences,
Grimaud is first in the queue,
With such a wonderful view.

For taking in these panoramas,
No need for pyjamas,
As with a telescope you can administer over the harbour,
Conducting square riggers from disaster,
All from your own terrace,
In splendid luxuriant laziness.

The walk to the piscine,
Is a ridiculous sojourn,
Nearly seventeen steps in between,
Heat avoidance and poolgasm.

MORAL *Go slow in Grimaud.*

DIARRHOEA

No compendium of Imodium,
No exotic probiotics,
No China Clay from a Cornishman,
No grade A narcotics,
Are you going to stem the flow,
So why not just let it go.

A simple walk around Stonehenge,
Can be subsumed by Monte Zuma's revenge,
You know when you have the trots,
The solstice - huh, I care not one jot!

A sudden tightening of the jowls,
Is easily offset by relaxing the bowels,
Indeed as this verse is being composed,
I'm afraid dear reader I've got to go,
There are cramps in the nether regions,
It's another bout of the damned Norwegians!

MORAL *To ensure best results: Eat rarish goat curry and plenty of white hot chilli.*

CIGAR

What often makes a wife shout out,
Is her husband's ability to flout,
Indeed show a total disregard,
For Doctor's orders about cigars.

You have to be an exceptional earner,
To acquire these devastating burners,
Firing one up takes several goes,
Before one can chomp through a Monte Christo.

So why do wives get in a huff,
Just because of a measly husband's puff?
Surely just a small amount of ash,
Cannot prevent the bedroom dash.

I'm told dear reader that it is the stench,
That prevents consummation with the wench,
And what knocks off all the bails,
Is when your husband exhales!

For a festival of smells escape the lips,
And rather deflates the bits between the hips,
As wafts of stale burnt tobacco,
Disrupt any thought of fellatio.

So what started as thoughts sublime,
With even the fleeting glimpse of a sixty nine,
Leads to disgruntled shaking of the heads,
And invariably dispassionate separate beds.

MORAL *Don't smoke.*

THINGS TO DO WITH A
HIRE CAR IN CORFU

Maps in Greece are prepared solely to guide you to where you can spend your money. Big red road, equals you can spend your money all along here and yes we need many of your Euros please.

So far you've trundled your Nissan Micra to the shops a few times and maybe a trip to Kassiopi harbour, where you cannot park unless you can exit the car through the boot, but Miss Micra and I had never done anything ambitious together. Indeed we had parted company for good at the mini roundabout in Kassiopi, when the gearstick came clean away from the gearbox. The patient man in the car behind, in addition to using full beam, horn and abuse, gave me no alternative; I got out of the car and showed him my knob.

By week two, Miss M and I had made up. We had done the ghastly trip to Aqualand, where Daddy had left a large portion of his buttocks on an upturned screw in the plastic sheeting. We had picked up vomiting teenagers at 4.30 in the morning, indeed we had even had a smoke together, when my loose end blew back into the rear seat and set fire to Miss Micra's lycra. Now we eyed each other in the driveway, her thin angular and slightly smashed headlights looked mournfully at me.

"What are we going to do to-day?" she winked, so I got out the map.

There were many good reasons for us to elope. Eight days of self-inflicted teenage carnage meant that complete peace had finally settled over the villa. They were all asleep. Also the old man of the Olive Press restaurant in Nissaki had confided in me;

"Go to Mont Pantokrator, great view, go see!"

Mount Pantokrator is the highest point in Corfu at some 918 meters. A yellow colour is allocated to this road, which means slightly terrifying blind bends. Perhaps the best reason yet for the trip was that a fire had started close to the top and it seemed a good idea to pull up, hopefully not off, Miss M's handbrake and view the spectacle from a safe distance. We started up the yellow road, when within 200 meters of the summit the great view was blocked by a large 11 year old in a day-glo jacket who jumped out in front of the car and asked us for ten euros.

"You park here, you pay, you walk."

Do you know what, there was no fire either. We turned about sharply, much to the yout's disappointment and headed for home disconsolate, but it had got me thinking. The Micra's handling was rigid in a straight line but unpredictable around a blind bend at 20mph. What would she be like off road?

The map had a barely discernible dotted black line which petered out before Pallies Sinies, left deserted over 500 years ago when sacked by the Saracen pirates. We had to see this! A sharp right took us down the dusty track as indicated on the map, through threadbare olive groves. We picked up speed billowing out a spectacular dust cloud, billowing as it happened over a very large bald man with tattoos and an Alsatian wolf dog on a chain for a lead. If one were to summarise the fleeting look on his face, it would be; "this was his place, cars never go this way, while I am consumed in a dust cloud, you'll have to turn around when the road runs out, which will enable my Alsatian to kill you, while I eat the Micra."

I gave him one of those "afternoon" half nods the English make when in real danger, leaving ironclad to do battle with the dust cloud. Perhaps the Alsatian would choke to death.

The incline was now about a one in eight in old money, gravel and jagged rocks replacing the dust track and the road had noticeably narrowed. Sounding nervous as her driver double de clutched over sheer rocky outcrops, we burst out of the scrub into a large quarry. Consoling myself that the view from the top would be so much better than from Pantokrator, and that it would be free, I swung my legs out of the car, groping around in my top pocket for a cheeky cigarette. It was nearly my last. The drop below Miss M's driver's door was about 250 meters! Our options were limited - okay, two.

We could press on or turnaround to face dinner with dusty tattoo man.

Driven by fear we carried on. We were now driving around the side of the mountain on the old Panies Sinies sheep and goat trail.

Water erosion had eaten into the rock, which jutted out in angular peaks in front of us. We should have turned back but we couldn't. The only turning circle was thin air and risking a 48 point turn overlooking this monumental escarpment seemed suicidal. On the Micra's chassis scraped and shrieked as we somehow clambered over dried water courses, wet gullies and razor sharp ridges. It had got to the stage where I had seriously begun thinking of abandoning her. Like a scared teenager after his first proper fumble, running away into the dusk, throwing the key onto the car hire desk minus car, and saying sorry the Micra had broken down, no, sorry I didn't know quite where and yes I was a silly old banana.

We stalled violently and I yanked the handbrake which thankfully responded by not parting company with the rest of the vehicle.
We were in real trouble, no phone, seven euros, and stuck with the sun setting on an obscure Z road which a Range Rover might have devoured, had there been enough width. We coasted backwards, took a pause for breath, and made a charge for the summit. Rocks exploded around us, Miss M raised her skirts, her tummy scraping the ridge line, sending a jarring screech through the length of her chassis as we summitted. She had done it and the view over the Agni peninsular was spectacular, our villa a faint white block in the middle distance.

We rolled downwards through the deserted village, passing an old gaol, a boarding house, a picturesque square, all light up by Miss M's sturdy beam. It was eerie, no people, lights, dogs, not even a cricket, just Miss M's little 1.1 litre engine spluttering after her exertions.
We coasted down the smooth snake like silky tarmac to Agni.

Oh and what of the fire? I had quite forgotten too. We rounded the bend to be met by a congregation of day-glo jacketed people. From a distance I thought they were more youts trying to extract more euros, but on closer examination they turned out to be about 20 prostrate firemen, smoking heavily, exhausted by their own exertions, lying blackened by the side of the road. We bumped over their lifeless firehoses and paddled into the villa victorious.

"Daddy where were you?" our daughter asked curtly.

"Around a new bit of the island, darling"

"What was it like?"

"A bit bumpy darling, quite fun actually."

I hadn't the heart to tell her that Miss M and I were actually quite lucky to be alive.

MORAL *Hire a boat.*

LECH'S TALK ABOUT
ZUHR AILMENTS

When you're skiing with the A team,
Bin the C team, they're not up to much,
OK yes, rather mean,
But honestly, broken helmets and a split crotch?

When you're coming down a long straight black,
Apparently there's no turning back,
Why not stop and linger,
Scratch your fly with a gangrenous finger.

Other ailments; well take your pick,
Try four bottles of Pinot Noir,
Without being remotely sick.

Others can go and perm their pelmet,
Be daft enough; wear a pink helmet,
Some say it's best to wear a vest,
A forty nine inch chest from Jess is best.

If you ever get to over fifty,
With the odd wrinkle up your crevasse,
Try being really thrifty,
Stick it on the front of your Versace.

Also if you're constantly feeling Tracy,
Dressed in tight pink and lacy,
Try one of her yogic modules,
That will bring out many globules.

If you wish to go out with an Arctic explorer,
Try by wearing an unusual fedora,
Just slip one in your pocket,
At anytime he can simply socket.

So no more mention of itchy chlamydia,
Broken shoulders, fingers or other bits of yer,
As passing ailments are of no concern,
Which is why my other villa is in Lucerne.

MORAL *Skiing is believing.*

FATHERS' AND SONS' SKI TRIP

Cometh the hour, cometh the Dad,
Their charges showing no fear,
Some ski sick, some ski bad,
We're off to the Mayers' layer.

Tubes, trains, taxis and planes,
Propelled us up the mountain,
No time for stopping or growing pains,
But time for some bedroom jousting.

Next morning we awoke to a clear blue void,
"Must be the time to try and brake a scaphoid,"
Said William executing a double twist,
Most successfully breaking his wrist.

"Gor blimey" shouted the unflappable Xander,
"It's looking like the battlefield at Flanders!",
And worse it became after many rosé infusions,
As unsteady fathers somersaulted into sparkly cushions.

Three Toms' Field, Williams and Wainwright,
Flew down mountains, goodness they kept it tight,
Birthday boy William showing considerable flare,
Becoming the world's fastest backward skier.

A prize also for an early starter,
Hanging fast and loose - Jack Carter,
And if anyone can O'Callaghan can,
And look, Hugo can can-can too!

Now when all was peace, serenity and calm,
Four excited bigger boys crept out to Animal Farm,
"Four double vodka red bulls please,"
Helped put us all at ease.

I daresay Prince Andrew was a little bereft,
To have vodka red bull thrown over his chest,
But to be fair he said "My name's Andrew..."
To which James said, "My name's Andrew too!"

And now real thanks where thanks is due,
And dear Peter this could be you,
You've put us all through our paces,
Made us all ski like aces,
Toboggan down from town to town,
And get us back to all our bases.

MORAL *When using a toboggan, never wear a sporran,*
As after a few groans and grunts, apparently it stays in your 'Y' fronts.

WHAT HAPPENS IF YOU DRINK THREE ESPRESSO MARTINI'S?

Thighs aching, back breaking; let's get to lunch,
Get stuck in to a small rum punch,
But not for our hostess Miss if you knew Susie 'Glaisher',
Was she going to get plastered and totally off her face,
No she was going to stay stone cold sober; hip hip hooray,
Then it landed; an ice coated frosted glass of Provence rosé.

And all she said was:
"I'll just have one
and when I'm done
Best get back fast and fed
and spring into my voluptuous bed."

For those of you who have led a life of solace
You know only too well she was talking bollocks.

So we changed for dinner as always required
Feeling replete considered joining a choir.

While in the half light, crouched in a grisly backstreet,
Miss Miller and Mrs Glaisher were shooting up a treat,
Syringing there oesophagi with inbetweenies,
Enormous no holes barred, espresso martinis.

The results are really hard to conceive,
And its certain, they were impossible to retrieve.
They bounced on beds like trampolines,
Susie's head firstly hit the ceiling.
With grudging admiration it then hit the door
Surrendering senseless the head finally collided with the floor.

MORAL *Sometimes three collects a crowd.*

THE RETURN HOME

If you want to screw up a great holiday, just try returning to one of
London's airports.
No we are not expecting all the flags out,
Red carpet treatment and free cigarette handouts,
Just a relaxed return, with a short meander,
Through passport control and into Alan's Panda.

For London Stansted, (Standstill is a better name),
Everyone says why drive there, let the train take the strain,
But good folk it's a hell of a palaver
Taking trollies trains and taxis, as frankly we rather,
Submit to the turmoil of the M25,
Of course it is easier to drive...

Parking in the midst of roadworks trying to remember space, 12 row Z, zone B,
It's worse than The Times crossword trying to retrieve the family.

For screwing up a perfectly good holiday retreat,
Then Gatwick is hard to beat,
It's not the atmosphere, the queues or the broken trolly,
Or the misery of the return with almost zero lolly,
It's your daughter's look of abject horror,
As the remains of her suitcase unravel on the conveyor.

Just because it's the smallest bag in Gatwick,
Covered in flowers and pink lipstick,
There was just no need to depth charge our daughter's emotions,
By undertaking quite so many controlled explosions,
Perhaps it was the collected seaside rubble,
That had identified this tiny suitcase for trouble.

And last but by no means least,
Without any conceivable thought to please,
Comes the very lowest of the low,
That unloved catacomb of the people that is Heathrow.

So T5 is the new place to be,
No one has thought about terminals one two or three,
The walls are peeling,
The laggings out the ceiling,
If these are cathedrals for travel,
Then stay at home and play some scrabble.

The British Army's national charity since 1944

soldierscharity.org

ABF The Soldiers' Charity is the national charity of the British Army, providing a lifetime of support to soldiers, veterans and their immediate families when they are in need. In the past year, we have helped 70,000 people in 68 countries across the globe and funded numerous charities and organisations to support the Army family at large. We pride ourselves on acting immediately when help is needed, providing true through-life support for the nation's soldiers, veterans and families. Crucially, we act with speed. When we are alerted that a person or family is in need of help, we aim to make the relevant grant within 48 hours. The Soldiers' Charity is most grateful to David Williams and his *Ghastly Holidays* for the donation of £1 per book sold to our charity.

To make a donation please visit:
www.soldierscharity.org